The Old Testament

PUZZLE BOOK

The Old Testament
PUZZLE BOOK

KIMIKO CHRISTENSEN HAMMARI

CFI
Springville, Utah

ISBN 13: 978-1-59955-368-9

Published by CFI, an imprint of Cedar Fort, Inc., 2373 W. 700 S., Springville, UT, 84663
Distributed by Cedar Fort, Inc., www.cedarfort.com

Cover design by Angela D. Olsen

Printed in the United States of America

10 9 8 7 6 5 4 3 2 1

Printed on acid-free paper

contents

all about the old testament

secret code

THEMES

Using the key below, decode the words on the following page to discover some of the themes of the Old Testament. ***Solution on page 84.***

A = ♋	J = ♉	S = ⬩
B = ♌	K = 😐	T = ⧫
C = ♍	L = ●	U = 💧
D = ♎	M = ❍	V = ❖
E = ♏	N = ■	W = ◎
F = ♐	O = □	X = ✠
G = ♑	P = ◻	Y = ⍓
H = ♒	Q = ❑	Z = ⌘
I = ♓	R = ❒	

1. ♌●♏⬧⬧♓■♑⬧ ___ ___ ___ ___ ___ ___ ___ ___ ___

2. ♍□❖♏■♋■⧫⬧ ___ ___ ___ ___ ___ ___ ___ ___ ___

3. ♐♋♓⧫♒ ___ ___ ___ ___ ___

4. ♐♋●● ___ ___ ___ ___

5. ♓♎□●♋⧫❑⍓ ___ ___ ___ ___ ___ ___ ___ ___

6. ●□⍓♋●⧫⍓ ___ ___ ___ ___ ___ ___ ___

7. ❍♋❑❑♓♋♑♏ ___ ___ ___ ___ ___ ___ ___ ___

8. □♌♏♎♓♏■♍♏ ___ ___ ___ ___ ___ ___ ___ ___ ___

9. ◻❑□◻♒♏♍⍓ ___ ___ ___ ___ ___ ___ ___ ___

10. ⬧♋♍❑♓♐♓♍♏ ___ ___ ___ ___ ___ ___ ___ ___ ___

word search

BOOKS, PART 1

Below is a list of the books found in the first half of the Old Testament. Find them in the word search to the right. Words appear forward, backward, and horizontally. ***Solution on page 86.***

GENESIS
EXODUS
LEVITICUS
NUMBERS
DEUTERONOMY
JOSHUA
JUDGES
RUTH
SAMUEL
KINGS
CHRONICLES
EZRA
NEHEMIAH
ESTHER
JOB
PSALMS
PROVERBS
ECCLESIASTES

K	I	N	G	S	H	P	G	O	S	H	G	J	U	F
P	S	S	R	J	I	C	X	Y	P	T	X	T	T	Y
S	B	R	E	O	F	S	S	T	C	U	J	X	J	M
L	R	E	A	L	O	T	E	Q	G	R	W	S	H	T
A	E	B	Y	S	C	W	E	N	X	N	L	U	A	O
M	V	M	Q	E	R	I	M	H	E	G	B	M	I	S
S	O	U	H	K	X	Z	N	G	C	G	Z	J	M	M
Z	R	N	W	Y	M	O	N	O	R	E	T	U	E	D
J	P	H	P	J	Y	L	D	R	R	H	H	D	H	E
B	A	B	Y	O	R	U	W	U	E	H	G	G	E	P
Q	L	E	O	B	K	S	U	P	S	H	C	E	N	M
B	U	S	U	C	I	T	I	V	E	L	T	S	S	M
L	E	U	M	A	S	W	V	N	Y	J	Z	S	R	V
H	X	G	E	C	C	L	E	S	I	A	S	T	E	S
G	A	R	Z	E	K	I	J	O	S	H	U	A	K	R

word search

BOOKS, PART 2

Below is a list of the books found in the second half of the Old Testament. Find them in the word search to the right. Words appear forward, backward, and horizontally. ***Solution on page 86.***

SONG OF SOLOMON
ISAIAH
JEREMIAH
LAMENTATIONS
EZEKIEL
DANIEL
HOSEA
JOEL
AMOS
OBADIAH
JONAH
MICAH
NAHUM
HABAKKUK
ZEPHANIAH
HAGGAI
ZECHARIAH
MALACHI

E J Z O O Q T G D H S G J D J

Z U I G A M O S T A O T D O Q

N V J C D H O S E A N I E X M

A W J I S A I A H D G I G G A

H Z E P H A N I A H O H E W L

U T J E J H R V H A F A O L A

M I D H Z B D C O F S B B N C

R F J E R E M I A H O A A L H

U O V J C W K F G J L K D K I

M I C A H L E I Q O O K I A D

R R N B L I C S E E M U A V K

P Z V J O N A H A L O K H M D

M Z E C H A R I A H N T F G O

L A M E N T A T I O N S R F Q

R C C N V J M I H A G G A I P

missing vowels

WHO WROTE THESE BOOKS?

The names of the first five books of the Old Testament appear below. However, all of the vowels are missing. Fill in the vowels that will complete each name. The missing vowels are below. Then unscramble the circled letters to discover who wrote these books. ***Solution on page 83.***

E E E E E E E   I I I

O O O   U U U U

---

1. G __ N __ (S) __ S
2. __ X __ D __ S
3. L __ V __ T __ C __ (S)
4. N __ M B (__) R S
5. D __ __ T __ R (__) N __ (M) Y

__ __ __ __ __

in the beginning

scripture puzzles

The puzzle below contains all the words to Genesis 1:27. Find the piece on the next page that correpsonds to each number and write the words from the puzzle piece in the spaces below. The first one has been done for you. When you are finished, read the words in order, from 1 to 17, to discover which scripture this puzzle contains. ***Solution on page 85.***

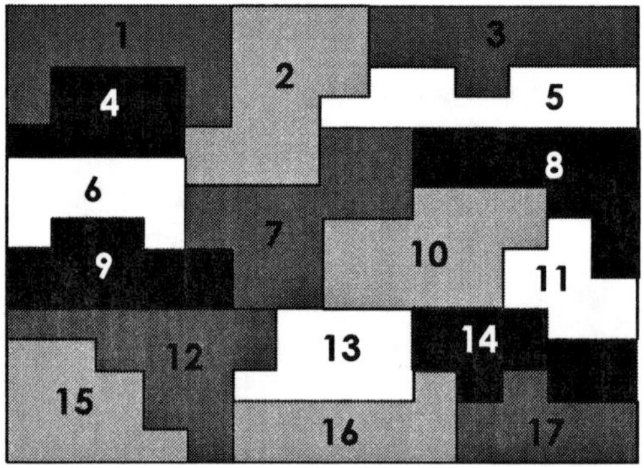

1. SO GOD
2.
3.
4.
5.
6.
7.
8.
9.
10.
11.
12.
13.
14.
15.
16.
17.

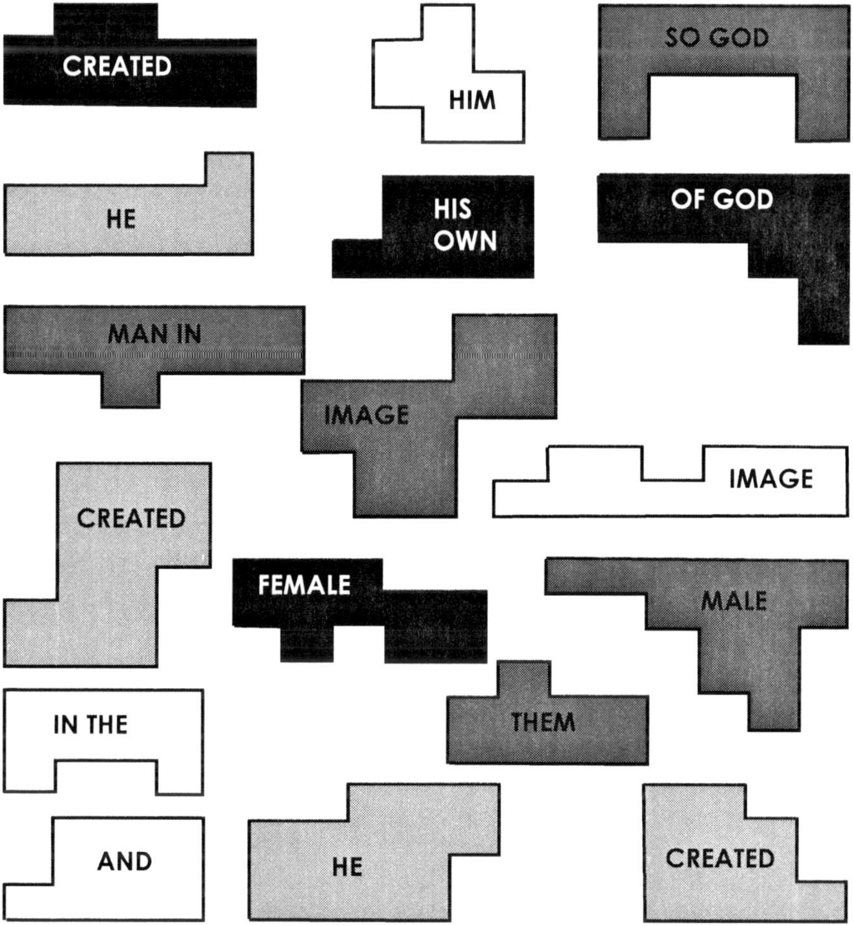
CREATED
HIM
SO GOD
HE
HIS OWN
OF GOD
MAN IN
IMAGE
CREATED
IMAGE
FEMALE
MALE
THEM
IN THE
AND
HE
CREATED

pick one

In each box, cross out all the words that are repeated until only one word remains. Place the remaining word on the blank line at the bottom of the page. After you have done this for each box, you will find the answer to clue below. ***Solution on page 84.***

THE TREE ADAM AND EVE WERE TOLD TO AVOID (GENESIS 2:16–17)

1

LEDGE	NOW	KNOW
EDGE	KNOWLEDGE	EDGE
KNOW	NOW	LEDGE

2

ON	OFT	OR
OFT	ON	ONE
ONE	OR	OF

3

GLAD	GO	GOOD
GOAT	GLOOM	GOAT
GLOOM	GO	GLAD

4

AND	APT	ARE
APE	ARE	ART
APE	ART	APT

5

DEVIL	LIVE	DEVIL
LIVER	EVIL	LIVER
LIVEN	LIVE	LIVEN

1. ____________ 2. ____________ 3. ____________

4. ____________ 5. ____________

hidden message

After the Flood, the Lord made a covenant with Noah and used a rainbow as a symbol of the covenant. Unscramble the words below to discover what the Lord promised Noah (and the rest of us). ***Solution on page 83.***

1. ______________________________
2. ______________________________
3. ______________________________
4. ______________________________
5. ______________________________

crossword puzzle

GENESIS 11: THE TOWER OF BABEL

Complete the crossword puzzle to the right by filling in the missing words from the verses below. For example, 2D in the verse below is the missing word that goes in 2 down, 10A is 10 across, and so forth. ***Solution on page 81.***

1 And the whole earth was of one (**1D**), and of one speech.

2 And it came to pass, as they journeyed from the (**3A**), that they found a plain in the land of Shinar; and they dwelt there.

3 And they said one to another, Go to, let us make (**6A**), and burn them throughly. And they had brick for stone, and (**8A**) had they for morter.

4 And they said, Go to, let us build us a city and a (**4D**), whose top may reach unto (**11A**); and let us make us a name, lest we be scattered abroad upon the face of the whole earth.

5 And the Lord came down to see the city and the tower, which the (**7D**) of men builded.

6 And the Lord said, Behold, the people is one, and they have all one language; and this they begin to do: and now nothing will be (**10A**) from them, which they have imagined to do.

7 Go to, let us go down, and there (**5D**) their language, that they may not understand one another's speech.

8 So the Lord (**2D**) them abroad from thence upon the face of all the (**9D**): and they left off to build the (**5A**).

9 Therefore is the name of it called (**6D**); because the Lord did there confound the language of all the earth: and from thence did the Lord scatter them abroad upon the face of all the earth.

1
2
3
4
5
6
7
8
9
10
11

word web

Follow the path below each letter until you reach the circle at the bottom of the page. Then write the letter in the circle. When you have done this for each letter, you will discover what Jesus made the first day of the Creation. ***Solution on page 85.***

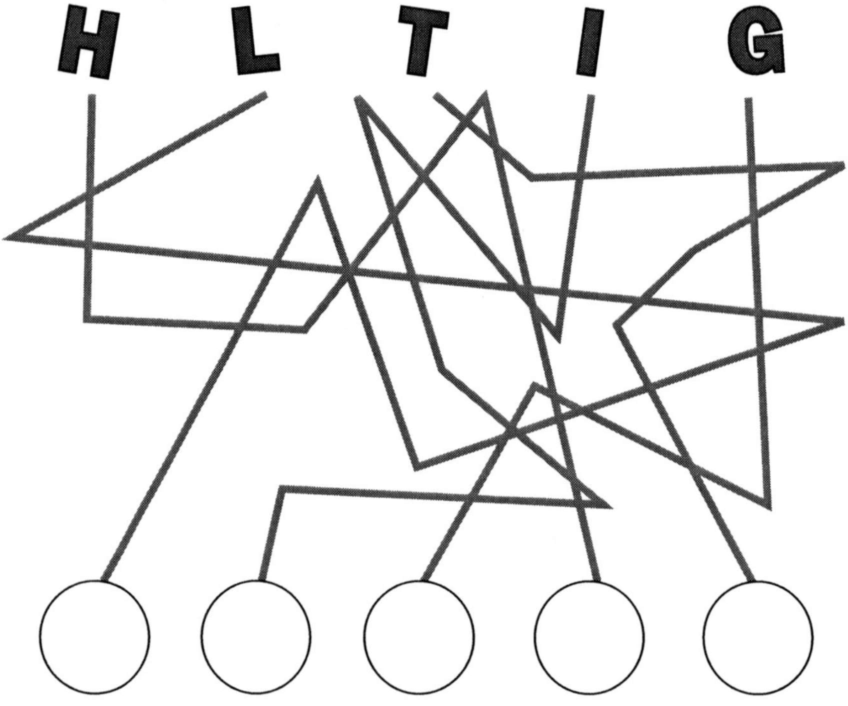

people/places

crossword puzzle

DANIEL 3: SHADRACH, MESHACH, AND ABED-NEGO

Complete the crossword puzzle to the right by filling in the missing words from the verses below. For example, 2A in the verse below is the missing word that goes in 2 across, 3D is 3 down, and so forth. ***Solution on page 81.***

23 And these three men, **(2A)**, Meshach, and Abed-nego, fell down bound into the midst of the burning fiery furnace.

24 Then Nebuchadnezzar the king was astonied, and rose up in haste, and spake, and said unto his counsellors, Did not we cast three men bound into the midst of the **(7A)**? They answered and said unto the king, True, O king.

25 He answered and said, Lo, I see **(7D)** men loose, walking in the midst of the fire, and they have no hurt; and the form of the fourth is like the Son of God.

26 Then Nebuchadnezzar came near to the mouth of the burning fiery **(11A)**, and spake, and said, Shadrach, Meshach, and Abed-nego, ye **(10D)** of the most **(4D)** God, come forth, and come hither. Then Shadrach, **(16A)**, and Abed-nego, came forth of the midst of the fire.

27 And the princes, governors, and captains, and the king's counsellors, being gathered together, saw these men, upon whose bodies the fire had no **(14A)**, nor was an **(9D)** of their head singed, neither were their coats changed, nor the **(2D)** of fire had passed on them.

28 Then Nebuchadnezzar spake, and said, **(6A)** be the God of Shadrach, Meshach, and **(1D)**, who hath sent his **(3D)**, and delivered his servants that trusted in him, and have changed the king's word, and yielded their bodies, that they might not **(8A)** nor **(5D)** any god, except their own God.

29 Therefore I make a **(13D)**, That every people, **(15A)**, and language, which speak any thing amiss against the God of Shadrach, Meshach, and Abed-nego, shall be cut in pieces, and their houses shall be made a dunghill: because there is no other **(12A)** that can deliver after this sort.

1
2
3
4
5
6
7
8
9
10
11
12
13
14
15
16

hangman

You'll need two or more players to play this game of hangman. Select one player to be the scribe, and the other player(s) will guess the phrase below. The scribe should look on page 82 to find the solution to the puzzle below.

LETTERS GUESSED

ABRAHAM PAID TITHING TO
THIS RIGHTEOUS KING

___ ___ ___ ___ ___ ___ ___ ___ ___ ___ ___

pick one

In each box, cross out all the words that are repeated until only one word remains. Place the remaining word on the blank line at the bottom of the page. After you have done this for each box, you will find the answer to clue below. ***Solution on page 84.***

WHAT JOSEPH TOLD HIS BROTHERS TO DO WHEN THEY TRIED TO BUY FOOD IN EGYPT (GENESIS 42)

1

BRIGHT	BRIDGE	BRIDE
BRING	BRIGHT	BROUGHT
BRIDGE	BRIDE	BROUGHT

2

ALSO	ALL	ALAS
ALTO	ALSO	ADO
ALAS	ADO	ALTO

3

TIE	THEN	TILE
THE	TIE	THY
THY	THEN	TILE

4

BROOM	BECOME	BROTHERS
BOTHERS	BROOM	BOTHER
BOTHERS	BOTHER	BECOME

5

TOT	TON	TOO
TON	TOT	TWO
TWO	TO	TOO

6

EGYPT	EIGHT	ENOUGH
ENOUGH	ENGLISH	EDEN
ENGLISH	EDEN	EIGHT

1. ____________ 2. ____________ 3. ____________

4. ____________ 5. ____________ 6. ____________

hangman

You'll need two or more players to play this game of hangman. Select one player to be the scribe, and the other player(s) will guess the phrase below. The scribe should look on page 82 to find the solution to the puzzle below.

LETTERS GUESSED

WHERE THE CITY OF ENOCH
WAS TAKEN

___ ___ ___ ___ ___ ___

word web

Follow the path below each letter until you reach the circle at the bottom of the page. Then write the letter in the circle. When you have done this for each letter, you will discover the name of the woman to whom Ruth pledged her loyalty. ***Solution on page 85.***

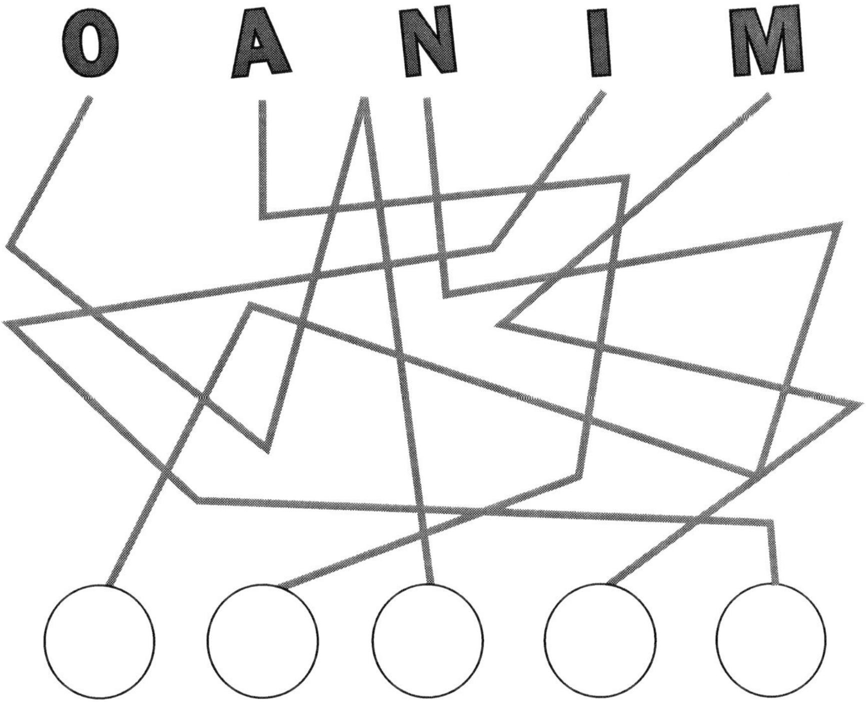

mix *n* match

Find the two pictures below and on the next page that are exactly the same. Then read the story of David and Goliath in 1 Samuel 17. ***Solution on page* 83.**

1

2

3

4

5

6

7

8

9

10

word web

Follow the path below each letter until you reach the circle at the bottom of the page. Then write the letter in the circle. When you have done this for each letter, you will discover the name of land where the Israelites lived as slaves. ***Solution on page 85.***

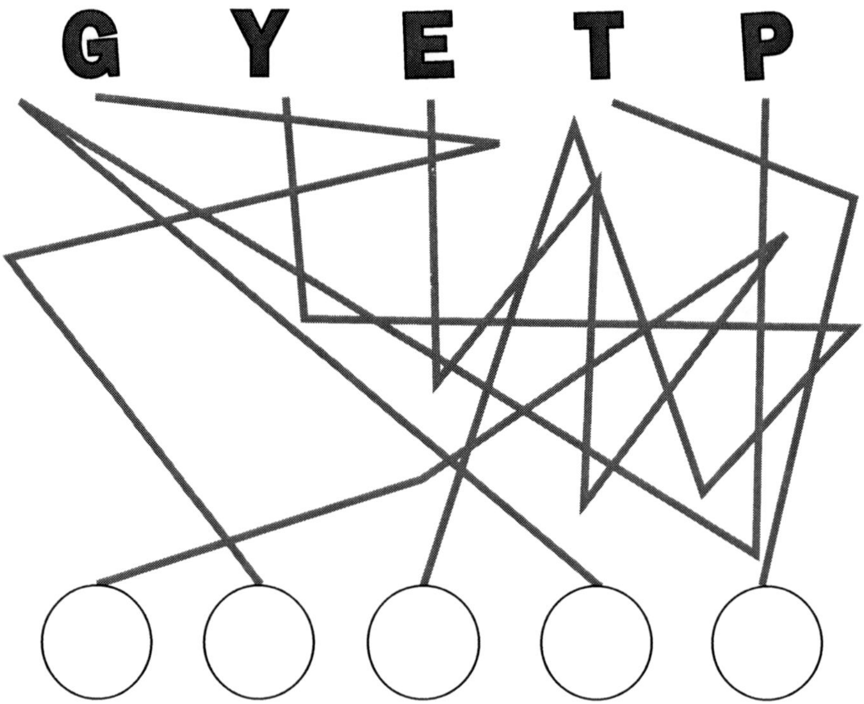

hangman

You'll need two or more players to play this game of hangman. Select one player to be the scribe, and the other player(s) will guess the phrase below. The scribe should look on page 82 to find the solution to the puzzle below.

LETTERS GUESSED

THREE DIFFERENT CITIES WHERE ABRAHAM LIVED

1. ___ ___

2 ___ ___ ___ ___ ___

3 ___ ___ ___ ___ ___ ___

missing vowels

12 TRIBES OF ISRAEL

The names of the 12 tribes of Israel appear on the following page. However, all of the vowels are missing. Fill in the vowels that will complete each name. The missing vowels are below. ***Solution on page 83.***

A A A A A A A A E E E E E E E E E

I I I I I O O U U U U

1. ___ S H ___ R

2. B ___ N J ___ M ___ N

3. D ___ N

4. G ___ D

5. ___ S S ___ C H ___ R

6. J ___ S ___ P H

7. J ___ D ___ H

8. L ___ V ___

9. N ___ P H T ___ L ___

10. R ___ ___ B ___ N

11. S ___ M ___ ___ N

12. Z ___ B ___ L ___ N

word search

PEOPLE

Below is a list of some of the people mentioned in the Old Testament. Find them in the word search to the right. Words appear forward, backward, diagonally, and horizontally. ***Solution on page 86.***

AARON
ABEL
ABSALOM
CAIN
DAVID
DELILAH
ELIAS
EVE
GOLIATH
HANNAH
ISAAC
JETHRO
LEAH
NAOMI
NOAH
RUTH
RACHEL
SAMUEL
SAUL

W	L	J	D	S	S	I	C	A	I	N	R	M	R	S
A	E	M	A	A	A	X	T	C	H	M	A	V	I	C
U	H	W	O	G	V	M	O	T	T	L	O	E	S	H
F	C	A	I	G	P	I	U	E	R	L	Y	S	A	M
H	A	N	N	A	H	R	D	E	X	E	Q	O	A	U
P	R	X	N	Q	L	A	M	W	L	B	N	W	C	G
W	G	M	Z	A	M	Z	I	N	S	A	O	D	N	M
I	J	V	D	X	S	N	E	A	W	K	E	O	O	I
E	C	L	E	N	Y	U	U	O	B	L	R	L	H	I
V	Z	P	L	A	N	L	V	L	I	A	A	V	T	G
E	X	K	U	O	O	W	T	L	A	S	I	Z	A	P
F	W	D	C	M	Q	W	A	D	B	P	D	U	I	E
Q	W	F	F	I	C	H	C	A	G	S	A	I	L	E
W	L	Z	H	A	E	L	O	L	Y	X	S	H	O	J
P	I	M	U	O	R	H	T	E	J	L	R	H	G	O

scripture puzzles

The puzzle below contains all the words to Isaiah 53:3 Find the piece on the next page that correpsonds to each number and write the words from the puzzle piece in the spaces below. The first one has been done for you. When you are finished, read the words in order, from 1 to 15, to discover which scripture this puzzle contains. ***Solution on page 85.***

1. He is
2.
3.
4.
5.
6.
7.
8.
9.
10.
11.
12.
13.
14.
15.

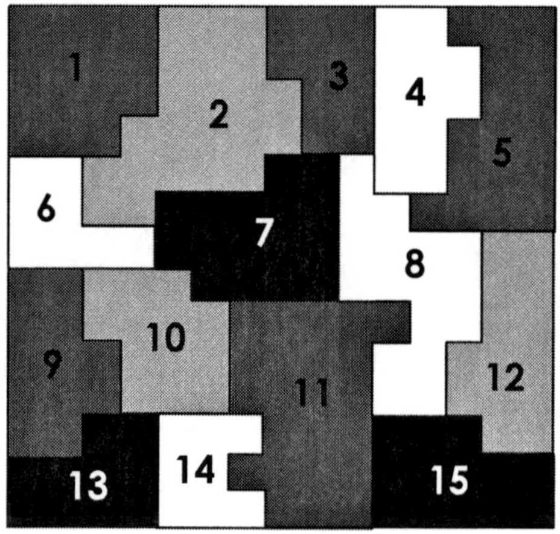

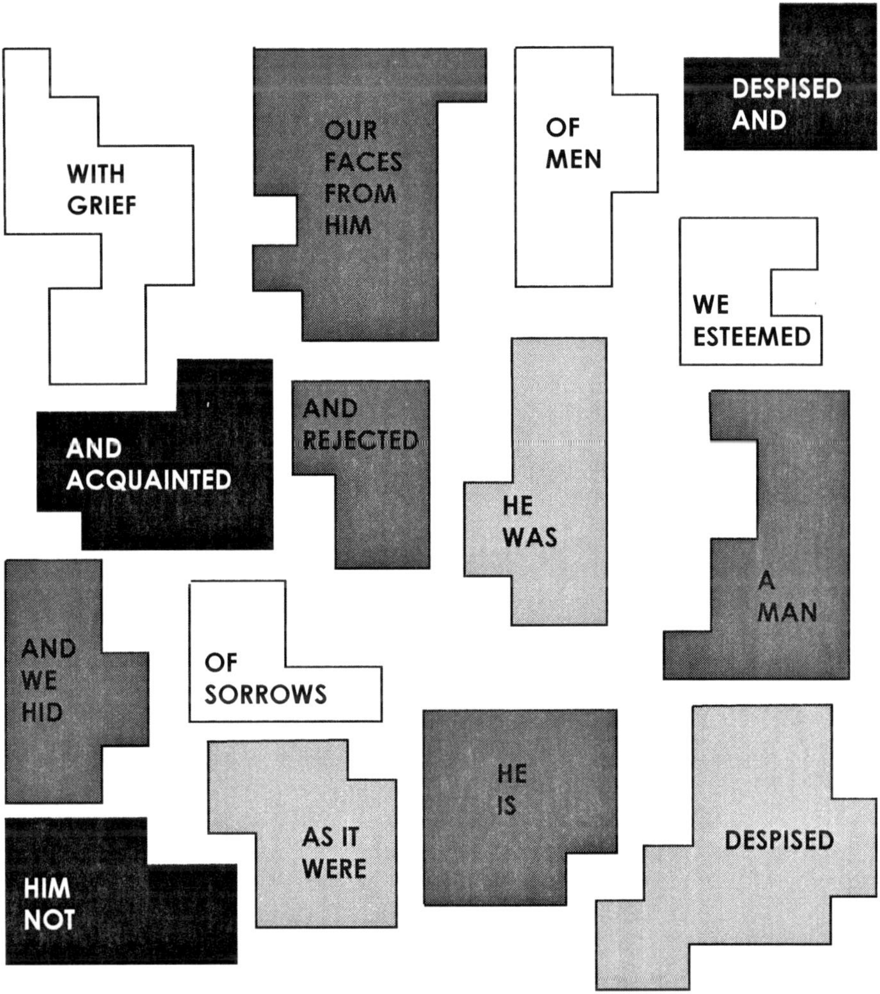
WITH GRIEF
OUR FACES FROM HIM
OF MEN
DESPISED AND
WE ESTEEMED
AND ACQUAINTED
AND REJECTED
HE WAS
A MAN
AND WE HID
OF SORROWS
HE IS
AS IT WERE
DESPISED
HIM NOT

word web

Follow the path below each letter until you reach the circle at the bottom of the page. Then write the letter in the circle. When you have done this for each letter, you will discover the name of the river that Joshua led the Israelites across to the promised land. ***Solution on page 85.***

hangman

You'll need two or more players to play this game of hangman. Select one player to be the scribe, and the other player(s) will guess the phrase below. The scribe should look on page 82 to find the solution to the puzzle below.

LETTERS GUESSED

ISAAC'S TWINS

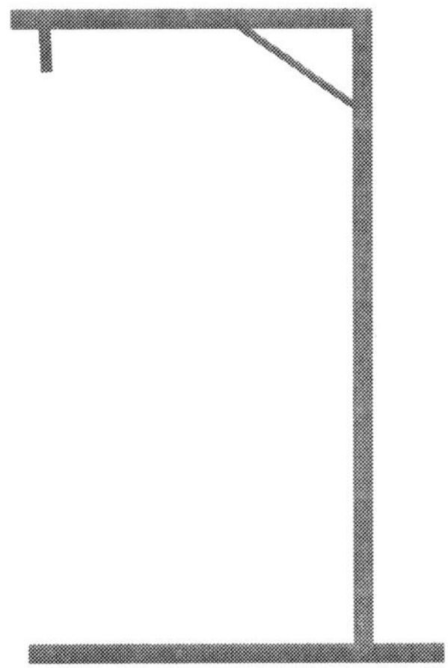

____ ____ ____ ____ ____

____ ____ ____

____ ____ ____ ____

word search

PLACES

Below is a list of some of the places mentioned in the Old Testament. Find them in the word search to the right. Words appear forward, backward, diagonally, and horizontally. ***Solution on page 86.***

BABYLON
BETHLEHEM
CANAAN
EARTH
EGYPT
GARDEN OF EDEN
HEAVEN
ISRAEL
JERICHO
JERUSALEM
JORDAN RIVER
KINGDOM OF JUDAH
MOAB
MOUNT SINAI
NINEVEH
PROMISED LAND
RED SEA
UR

U	R	Y	W	T	I	B	H	B	B	S	O	Y	R	R
C	C	W	U	W	S	N	A	L	E	U	N	A	K	A
R	B	R	L	V	R	M	D	D	T	O	E	Z	X	I
D	E	B	U	R	A	Y	U	Q	H	Y	D	G	M	O
N	W	V	A	O	E	T	J	S	L	E	E	N	O	Z
A	D	O	I	B	L	B	F	S	E	A	F	I	A	N
L	G	O	A	R	Y	Z	O	O	H	R	O	N	B	Z
D	A	L	N	Y	N	L	M	N	E	T	N	E	B	V
E	C	J	I	O	G	A	O	H	M	H	E	V	I	V
S	N	E	S	X	C	R	D	N	Q	S	D	E	N	E
I	A	R	T	H	C	E	G	R	T	K	R	H	E	Z
M	A	I	N	S	W	D	N	G	O	Z	A	D	V	D
O	N	C	U	E	Y	S	I	U	Q	J	G	M	A	J
R	A	H	O	V	W	E	K	Z	T	P	Y	G	E	N
P	C	O	M	E	L	A	S	U	R	E	J	C	H	G

pick one

In each box, cross out all the letters that are repeated until only one remains. Place the remaining letter on the corresponding blank line at the bottom of the page. After you have done this for each box, you will find the answer to clue below. ***Solution on page 84.***

AN OLD TESTAMENT QUEEN

3

T	F	A	L	O
F	G	H	R	G
H	R	L	O	A

5

M	F	S	Q	K
K	G	W	Q	W
E	F	S	M	G

6

P	S	B	W	D
I	D	H	I	H
B	W	P	S	R

1

C	G	B	E	W
W	Y	G	V	H
H	V	Y	B	C

2

V	C	J	X	T
U	X	A	U	A
S	T	V	J	C

4

Y	S	T	N	Z
O	Z	E	O	E
T	S	Y	N	H

____ ____ ____ ____ ____ ____

1 2 3 4 5 6

commandments

crossword puzzle

EXODUS 20: THE 10 COMMANDMENTS

Complete the crossword puzzle to the right by filling in the missing words from the verses below. For example, 7A in the verse below is the missing word that goes in 7 across, 12D is 12 down, and so forth. ***Solution on page 81.***

3 Thou shalt have no other (**10A**) before
me.
4 Thou shalt not make unto thee any
graven image, or any (**14A**) of any thing
that is in heaven above, or that is in the
earth beneath, or that is in the water
under the earth:
5 Thou shalt not bow down thyself to
them, nor serve them. . . .
7 Thou shalt not take the name of the
Lord thy God in (**12D**); for the Lord will
not hold him (**13A**) that taketh his name
in vain.
8 Remember the (**2D**) day, to keep it
holy.
9 Six days shalt thou labour, and do all
thy work:
10 But the seventh day is the (**2A**) of the
Lord thy God: in it thou shalt not do any
work, thou, nor thy son, nor thy (**5A**), thy
manservant, nor thy maidservant, nor
thy cattle, nor thy stranger that is within
thy gates:
11 For in six days the Lord made heaven
and earth, the sea, and all that in them is,
and (**6D**) the seventh day: wherefore the
Lord blessed the sabbath day, and (**7A**) it.
12 Honour thy (**8A**) and thy mother:
that thy days may be long upon the land
which the Lord thy God giveth thee.
13 Thou shalt not (**4D**).
14 Thou shalt not commit (**3D**).
15 Thou shalt not (**11D**).
16 Thou shalt not bear false (**9D**)
against thy neighbour.
17 Thou shalt not (**1D**) thy neighbour's
house, thou shalt not covet thy
neighbour's wife, nor his manservant, nor
his maidservant, nor his ox, nor his ass,
nor any thing that is thy neighbour's.

1
2
3
4
5
6
7
8
9
10
11
12
13
14

pick one

In each box, cross out all the words that are repeated until only one word remains. Place the remaining word on the blank line at the bottom of the page. After you have done this for each box, you will find the answer to clue below. ***Solution on page 84.***

WHAT THE ISRAELITES DID DURING THE PASSOVER (EXODUS 12:7)

1

PUT	PUTT	PAT
PUTT	PIT	PET
PET	PAT	PIT

2

LAKES	LARKS	LAKES
LACES	LACE	LACES
LAMBS'	LARKS	LACE

3

BLOOD	BROOM	BLOOM
BLED	BLOOM	BOOM
BROOM	BOOM	BLED

4

OF	OR	ON
OFT	OF	OFF
OFT	OFF	OR

5

THERE	THEIR	THEY'RE
THINE	THEY'RE	THEN
THEN	THERE	THINE

6

FLOOR	DOOR	FLOORS
DOOR	FLOOR	FOUR
FOUR	DOORS	FLOORS

1. __________ 2. __________ 3. __________

4. __________ 5. __________ 6. __________

hangman

You'll need two or more players to play this game of hangman. Select one player to be the scribe, and the other player(s) will guess the phrase below. The scribe should look on page 82 to find the solution to the puzzle below.

LETTERS GUESSED

WHAT THE ISRAELITES WERE TOLD NOT TO WORSHIP

___ ___ ___ ___ ___ ___

___ ___ ___ ___

word search

MALACHI 3

Unscramble the words in the verses below and then find them in the word search to the right. Words appear forward, backward, and horizontally. ***Solution on page 87.***

8 Will a man **(1) BRO** God? Yet
ye have robbed me. But ye say,
Wherein have we robbed thee? In
(2) TSEIHT and **(3) FEFSNGIOR**.
9 Ye are cursed with a **(4) ECSUR**:
for ye have robbed me, even this
whole **(5) TANOIN**.
10 Bring ye all the tithes into the
(6) OETUSSHEOR, that there may be
(7) TEAM in mine **(8) USEOH**, and
(9) VORPE me now herewith, saith
the **(10) ROLD** of hosts, if I will not
open you the **(11) INODSWW** of
heaven, and **(12) ROUP** you out a
(13) BNSSGLISE, that there shall not
be **(14) MORO** enough to receive it.

1.
2.
3.
4.
5.
6.
7.
8.
9.
10.
11.
12.
13.
14.

Z B H K T I T H E S Z V O W K

D L T X T Z D D N A T I O N J

E E C G Z M H O U S E X F Y X

F S T O R E H O U S E X C Y W

H S X H T E H F T T S U B O I

K I Q Z Z Z R Y I W F W A F L

U N U V I U R O O M C X H F F

X G B R O H H D T W P V D E Y

U O A P O S N C A M R R O R Y

R K J F U I E C O E O Z M I B

P L F W W T Y F N W V V H N E

C F O J C U R S E S E K P G V

V Y H I B Z Z P L O R D C S O

E I X H Q Q W M E A T W K C S

S A X A G A B A S Q A I P U F

scripture puzzles

The puzzle below contains all the words in Leviticus 18:19. Find the piece on the next page that correpsonds to each number and write the words from the puzzle piece in the spaces below. The first one has been done for you. When you are finished, read the words in order, from 1 to 19, to discover which scripture this puzzle contains. ***Solution on page 85.***

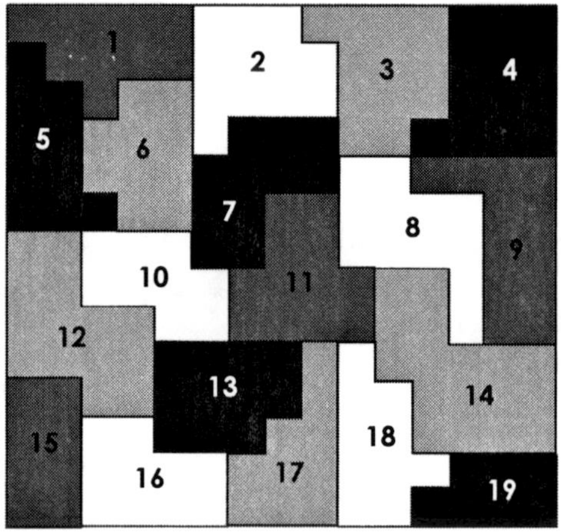

1. THOU
2.
3.
4.
5.
6.
7.
8.
9.
10.
11.
12.
13.
14.
15.
16.
17.
18.
19.

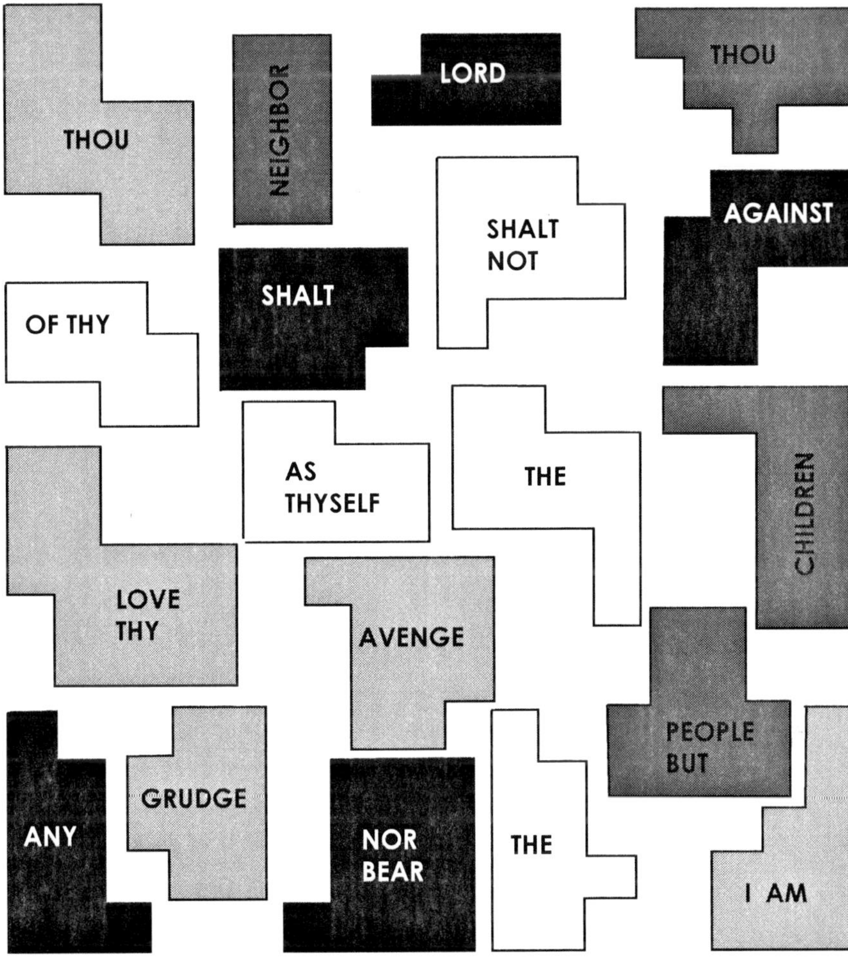
THOU
NEIGHBOR
LORD
THOU
SHALT NOT
AGAINST
OF THY
SHALT
AS THYSELF
THE
CHILDREN
LOVE THY
AVENGE
PEOPLE BUT
ANY
GRUDGE
NOR BEAR
THE
I AM

hangman

You'll need two or more players to play this game of hangman. Select one player to be the scribe, and the other player(s) will guess the phrase below. The scribe should look on page 82 to find the solution to the puzzle below.

LETTERS GUESSED

THE LORD COMMANDED MOSES
TO BUILD THIS

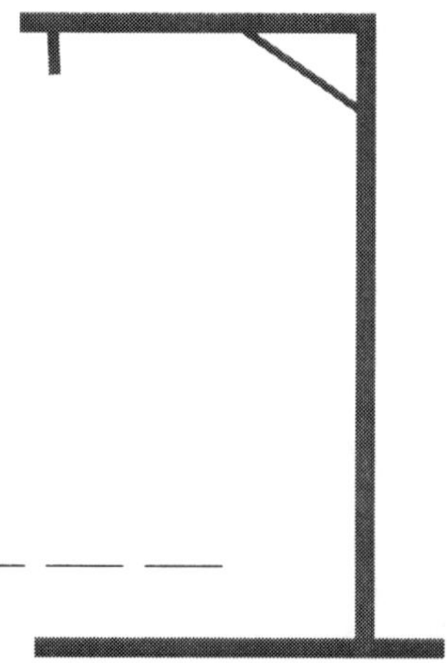

___ ___ ___ ___ ___ ___ ___ ___ ___ ___

prophets

crossword puzzle

EXODUS 2: BABY MOSES

Complete the crossword puzzle to the right by filling in the missing words from the verses below. For example, 4A in the verse below is the missing word that goes in 4 across, 6D is 6 down, and so forth. ***Solution on page 81.***

1 And there went a man of the house of Levi, and took to wife a daughter of **(13D)**.

2 And the woman conceived, and bare a son: and when she saw him that he was a goodly child, she hid him **(14A)** months.

3 And when she could not longer **(16A)** him, she took for him an ark of **(9A)**, and daubed it with slime and with pitch, and put the child therein; and she laid it in the flags by the river's brink.

4 And his **(11D)** stood afar off, to wit what would be done to him.

5 And the **(15A)** of Pharaoh came down to wash herself at the **(5D)**; and her maidens walked along by the river's side; and when she saw the ark among the flags, she sent her maid to fetch it.

6 And when she had opened it, she saw the **(12A)**: and, behold, the babe wept. And she had **(3D)** on him, and said, This is one of the Hebrews' children.

7 Then said his sister to Pharaoh's daughter, Shall I go and call to thee a **(4A)** of the **(6D)** women, that she may nurse the child for thee?

8 And Pharaoh's daughter said to her, Go. And the maid went and called the child's **(10A)**.

9 And Pharaoh's daughter said unto her, Take this child away, and nurse it for me, and I will give thee thy wages. And the woman took the **(8D)**, and nursed it.

10 And the child grew, and she brought him unto Pharaoh's daughter, and he became her **(2D)**. And she called his name **(1A)**: and she said, Because I drew him out of the **(7D)**.

hangman

You'll need two or more players to play this game of hangman. Select one player to be the scribe, and the other player(s) will guess the phrase below. The scribe should look on page 82 to find the solution to the puzzle below.

LETTERS GUESSED

PROPHET WHO SUCCEEDED
(CAME AFTER) MOSES

___ ___ ___ ___ ___ ___

dot-to-dot

Complete the dot-to-dot. Then read Jonah 1–3 to discover what this image represents.
Solution on page 83.

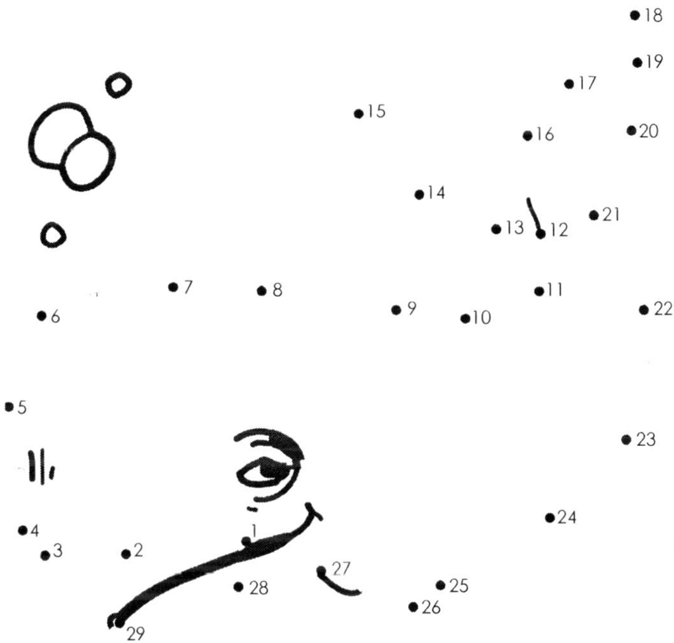

mix n match

Find the two pictures below and on the next page that are exactly the same. ***Solution on page 83.***

1

2

3

4

5

6

7

8

9

10

word search

DANIEL 2

Unscramble the words in the verses below and then find them in the word search to the right. Words appear forward, backward, diagonally, and horizontally. ***Solution on page 87.***

44 And in the days of these **(1) GNIKS**
shall the God of **(2) AEVHNE** set up
a kingdom, which shall **(3) EVERN** be
destroyed: and the kingdom shall not be left
to other **(4) OEPPEL**, but it shall break in
pieces and consume all these kingdoms, and
it shall **(5) TASND** for ever.
45 Forasmuch as thou sawest that the
(6) SENOT was cut out of the mountain
without **(7) NDSHA**, and that it brake in
pieces the iron, the brass, the **(8) LACY**,
the silver, and the **(9) DOLG**; the great
God hath made known to the king what
shall come to pass hereafter: and the
(10) RDEMA is certain, and the
interpretation thereof **(11) RUSE**.

1.

2.

3.

4.

5.

6.

7.

8.

9.

10.

11.

U	G	H	T	L	T	M	R	H	C	Y	Q	R	D	X
C	M	O	U	G	K	T	P	H	I	L	L	D	G	A
C	X	T	N	I	O	Z	Y	S	Y	W	A	C	Q	D
W	P	B	E	E	D	S	Y	O	P	M	E	Y	R	K
B	C	Z	L	X	V	R	G	O	L	D	O	N	A	U
Y	G	B	H	W	C	A	E	Z	S	C	W	N	R	B
U	S	S	U	R	E	S	E	A	W	C	Y	Q	A	V
T	Y	G	R	C	G	C	I	H	M	N	D	F	D	X
T	F	N	S	N	K	R	Y	B	V	L	J	N	V	G
S	U	I	I	P	O	Z	Y	M	Z	Q	A	V	S	G
D	W	K	Q	F	I	Y	Q	R	M	T	C	R	X	J
N	P	E	O	P	L	E	D	U	S	H	T	E	N	S
A	O	V	W	M	I	E	N	O	T	S	T	V	E	W
H	F	Y	L	Z	T	G	T	S	P	J	Y	E	U	M
C	N	N	L	N	L	S	I	X	S	T	K	N	Y	S

scripture puzzles

The puzzle below contains all the words to Amos 3:7. Find the piece on the next page that corresponds to each number and write the words from the puzzle piece in the spaces below. The first one has been done for you. When you are finished, read the words in order, from 1 to 17, to discover which scripture this puzzle contains. ***Solution on page 85.***

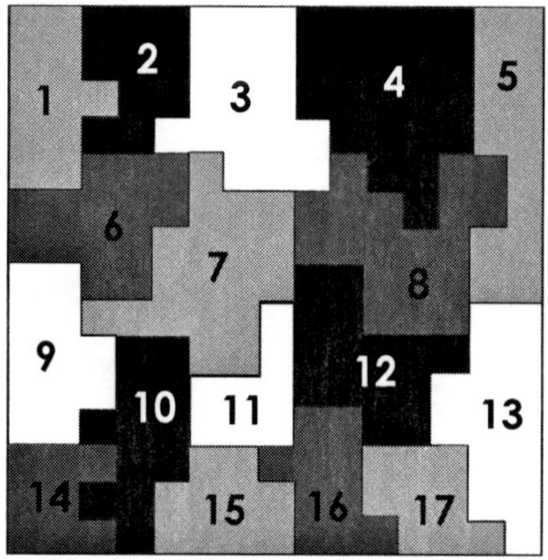

1. SURELY
2.
3.
4.
5.
6.
7.
8.
9.
10.
11.
12.
13.
14.
15.
16.
17.

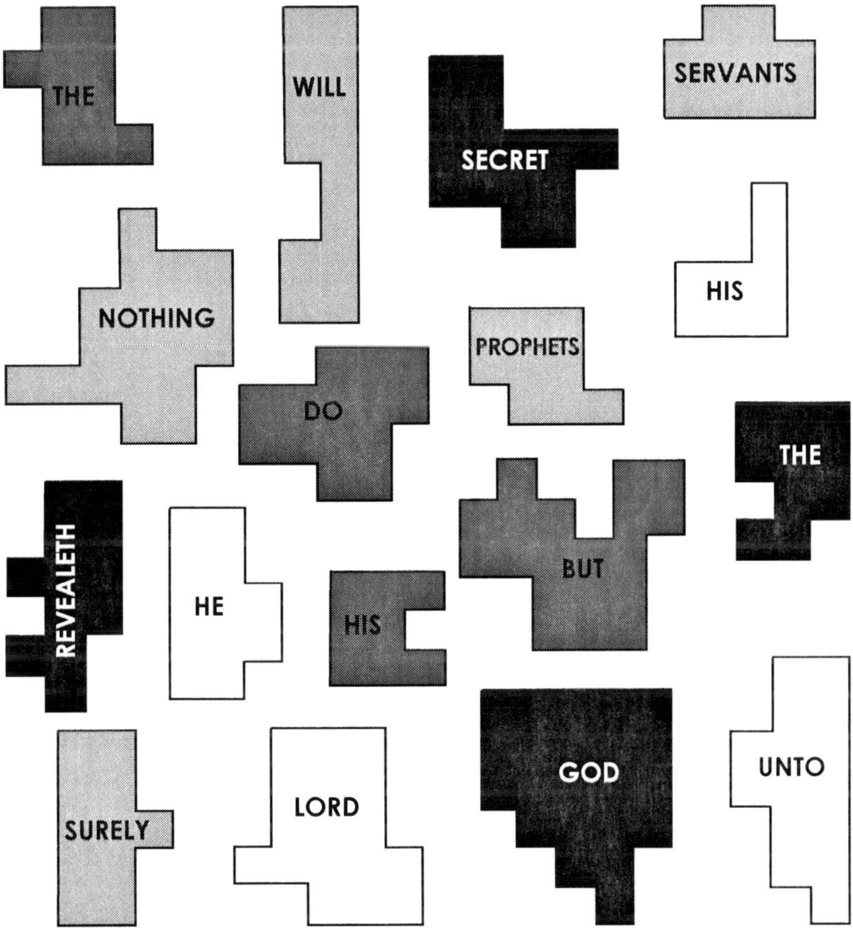
THE
WILL
SERVANTS
SECRET
HIS
NOTHING
PROPHETS
DO
THE
REVEALETH
HE
HIS
BUT
SURELY
LORD
GOD
UNTO

faith

crossword puzzle

DANIEL 6: DANIEL IN THE LION'S DEN

Complete the crossword puzzle to the right by filling in the missing words from the verses below. For example, 9A in the verse below is the missing word that goes in 9 across, 3D is 3 down, and so forth. ***Solution on page 82.***

16 Then the king commanded, and they brought (**10D**), and cast him into the (**11A**) of lions. Now the king spake and said unto Daniel, Thy God whom thou servest continually, he will (**1A**) thee.

17 And a stone was brought, and laid upon the mouth of the den; and the (**12A**) sealed it with his own signet, and with the signet of his lords; that the purpose might not be changed concerning Daniel. . . .

19 Then the king arose very early in the (**18A**), and went in haste unto the den of (**16D**).

20 And when he came to the den, he cried with a lamentable voice unto Daniel: and the king spake and said to Daniel, O Daniel, (**17A**) of the (**16A**) God, is thy God, whom thou servest continually, able to deliver thee from the lions?

21 Then said Daniel unto the king, O king, (**4A**) for ever.

22 My God hath sent his (**14D**), and hath shut the lions' (**15D**), that they have not hurt me: forasmuch as before him innocency was found in me; and also before thee, O king, have I done no hurt.

23 Then was the king exceeding glad for him, and (**9A**) that they should take Daniel up out of the den. . . .

25 Then king Darius wrote unto all people, (**7D**), and languages. . . .

26 I make a decree, That in every dominion of my kingdom men (**3D**) and fear before the God of Daniel: for he is the living God, and stedfast for ever, and his (**12D**) that which shall not be destroyed, and his dominion shall be even unto the (**5D**).

27 He delivereth and (**2D**), and he worketh signs and (**6A**) in heaven and in (**8D**), who hath delivered Daniel from the (**13A**) of the lions.

pick one

In each box, cross out all the words that are repeated until only one word remains. Place the remaining word on the blank line at the bottom of the page. After you have done this for each box, you will find the answer to clue below. ***Solution on page 84.***

HOW LONG HANNAH PROMISED HER SON WOULD SERVE THE LORD (1 SAMUEL 1:11)

1

AXE	ABLE	ALL
ARE	AND	ABLE
AND	ARE	AXE

2

TOE	TAN	TIE
TAN	TIE	THEE
THE	THEE	TOE

3

DRY	DYE	DRIES
DIE	DRIES	DYE
DAYS	DRY	DIE

4

ODE	OFT	ORE
OFT	OF	ODES
ODES	ORE	ODE

5

HIM	HER	HYMN
HYMN	HAS	HER
HAS	HIM	HIS

6

LIFE	LIVE	LIFT
LIVE	LIFT	LIST
LINE	LIST	LINE

1. ____________ 2. ____________ 3. ____________

4. ____________ 5. ____________ 6. ____________

everything else

crossword puzzle

1 KINGS 3: KING SOLOMON'S WISDOM

Complete the crossword puzzle to the right by filling in the missing words from the verses below. For example, 2A in the verse below is the missing word that goes in 3 across, 3D is 2 down, and so forth. ***Solution on page 82.***

16 Then came there two **(19A)** . . . unto the king, and stood before him.

17 And the one woman said, O my lord, I and this woman dwell in one **(16A)**; and I was delivered of a child with her in the house.

18 And it came to pass the **(2D)** day after that I was delivered, that this woman was delivered also: and we were together; there was no **(1A)** with us in the house, save we two in the house.

19 And this woman's **(15D)** died in the night; because she overlaid it.

20 And she arose at **(9D)**, and took my son from beside me, while thine handmaid slept, and laid it in her bosom, and laid her dead **(17A)** in my bosom.

21 And when I rose in the **(9A)** to give my child suck, behold, it was **(7A)**: but when I had considered it in the morning, behold, it was not my **(6D)**, which I did bear.

22 And the other woman said, Nay; but the **(4D)** is my son, and the dead is thy son. And this said, No; but the **(8D)** is thy son, and the living is my son. Thus they spake before the king. . . .

24 And the king said, Bring me a **(12A)**. And they brought a sword before the king.

25 And the king said, **(20A)** the living child in two, and give **(3A)** to the one, and half to the other.

26 Then spake the woman whose the **(14D)** child was unto the king, for her bowels yearned upon her son, and she said, O my lord, **(11D)** her the living child, and in no wise slay it. But the other said, Let it be neither mine nor thine, but **(5A)** it.

27 Then the king answered and said, Give her the living child, and in no wise slay it: she is the **(10D)** thereof.

28 And all **(18A)** heard of the judgment which the king had judged; and they feared the king: for they saw that the **(13D)** of **(11A)** was in him, to do judgment.

drawing from the scriptures

Each square below contains a piece of a bigger picture. Draw what you see from each box below in the empty box with matching coordinates. (An example has been done for you.) After you have finished the picture, read Numbers 22 to discover the signifiance of this animal. ***Solution on page 83.***

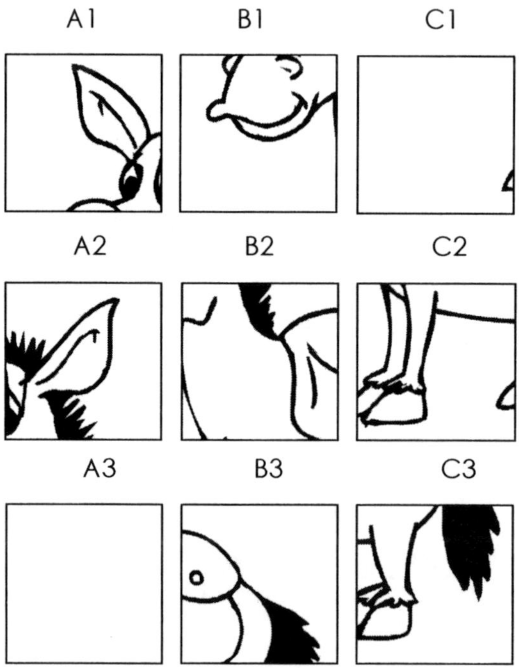

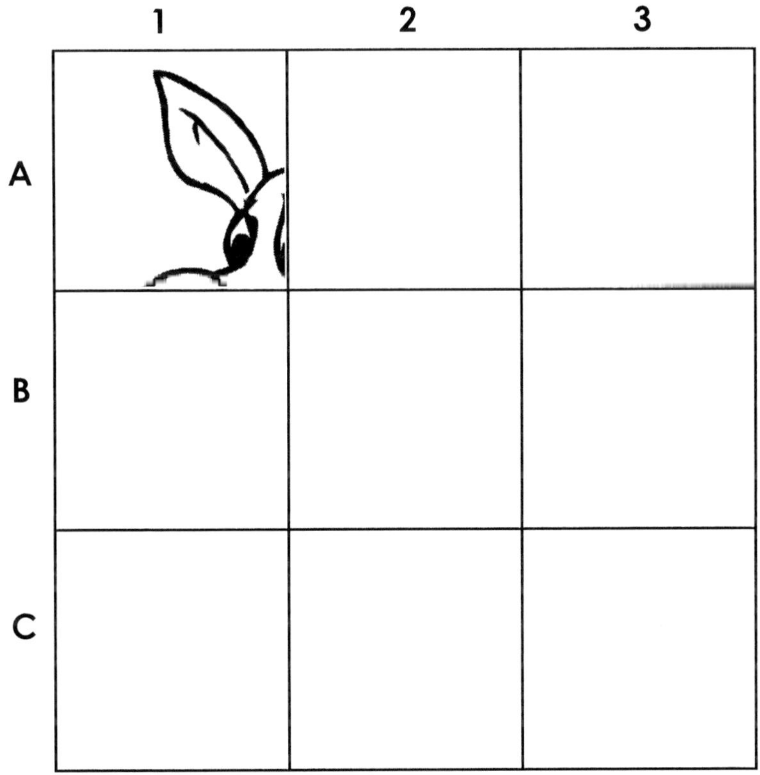
1
2
3
A
B
C

crossword puzzle

MALACHI 4

Complete the crossword puzzle to the right by filling in the missing words from the verses below. For example, 5A in the verse below is the missing word that goes in 5 across, 8D is 8 down, and so forth. ***Solution on page 82.***

1 For, behold, the (**15A**) cometh, that
shall burn as an (**12A**); and all the proud,
yea, and all that do wickedly, shall be
(**17A**): and the day that cometh shall
burn them up, saith the Lord of hosts,
that it shall leave them neither (**6A**) nor
branch.
2 But unto you that fear my name shall
the Sun of (**2A**) arise with (**13A**) in his
wings; and ye shall go forth, and grow up
as calves of the stall.
3 And ye shall tread down the (**8D**);
for they shall be ashes under the soles of
your feet in the day that I shall do this,
saith the (**14D**) of hosts.
4 Remember ye the law of (**11D**) my
servant, which I commanded unto him
in Horeb for all (**10D**), with the statutes
and judgments.
5 Behold, I will send you (**7D**) the
prophet before the coming of the great
and (**1D**) day of the Lord:
6 And he shall turn the (**16A**) of the
fathers to the (**4D**), and the heart of the
children to their (**5A**), lest I come and
(**9A**) the earth with a (**3D**).

1
2
3
4
5
6
7
8
9
10
11
12
13
14
S
15
16
17

scripture chase

JEREMIAH 16:16

This scripture chase is different from the ones you're used to. Instead of searching for scriptures in the Old Testament, you'll search for a scripture in this grid. Begin at the circled letter and draw a line through each letter of the word as you find it. Words read forward, backward, up, and down, but not diagonally. The first letter of each word is in bold. Don't skip any letters. Every letter in the grid will be used. Use the scripture below to find out which word to search for next. ***Solution on page 84.***

I WILL SEND FOR MANY FISHERS, SAITH THE LORD, AND THEY SHALL FISH THEM; AND AFTER WILL I SEND FOR MANY HUNTERS, AND THEY SHALL HUNT THEM FROM EVERY MOUNTAIN, AND FROM EVERY HILL, AND OUT OF THE HOLES OF THE ROCKS

I **W** O R **M** E M N T E R S **A** R Y

I I **F** N A H **A** U E H **T** D N E **M**

L N D Y H **T** N **H** Y R O M **E** V O

S E I **F** S **A** D Y **S** **F** M A T N U

F H S **F** I F A N H H E I O M **E**

R **S** H L E T **M** L A **T** **A** N R E V

S Y A L R O R L N T N D **F** R Y

S E H **T** **W** **F** D **H** U H **T** F **O** I **H**

A H E D I L N O **H** E **R** O T L L

I **T** **L** N **A** L E L **O** F E C U **O** **A**

T H O R D **I** **S** E S **T** H K S D N

scripture chase

PSALM 24:3–4

This scripture chase is different from the ones you're used to. Instead of searching for scriptures in the Old Testament, you'll search for a scripture in this grid. Begin at the circled letter and draw a line through each letter of the word as you find it. Words read forward, backward, up, and down, but not diagonally. The first letter of each word is in bold. Don't skip any letters. Every letter in the grid will be used. Use the scripture below to find out which word to search for next. ***Solution on page 84.***

WHO SHALL ASCEND INTO THE HILL OF THE LORD? OR WHO SHALL STAND IN HIS HOLY PLACE?
HE THAT HATH CLEAN HANDS, AND A PURE HEART; WHO HATH NOT LIFTED UP HIS SOUL UNTO VANITY, NOR SWORN DECEITFULLY.

N I T O **N** H T A H **W** A **H** N H **T**

A **N** Y T **L** I F **H** O T N D A A E

V O W O R N T E A R **A** S E T **H**

O R **S** L L **D** E D E D N **C** L **H** E

T N **U** U Y E C **U** **H** **A** **P** H T A C

L L L F T I **H** P E R U Y **P** L A

A **A** U O **S** S I H E **L** O L S I **H**

H S C N T O **T** **T** **O** D R O **H** **I** N

S O E **I** **H** E H F R O **S** L L D N

W H N D I L L **O** **W** H H A **S** T A

drawing from the scriptures

Each square below contains a piece of a bigger picture. Draw what you see from each box below in the empty box with matching coordinates. (An example has been done for you.) The completed picture represents one of the plagues Egypt suffered when Pharaoh refused to free the children of Israel. You can read about the plagues in Exodus 7–12. ***Solution on page 83.***

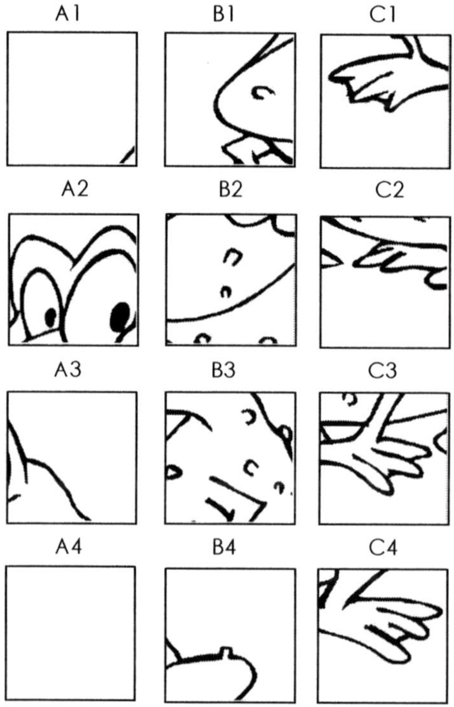

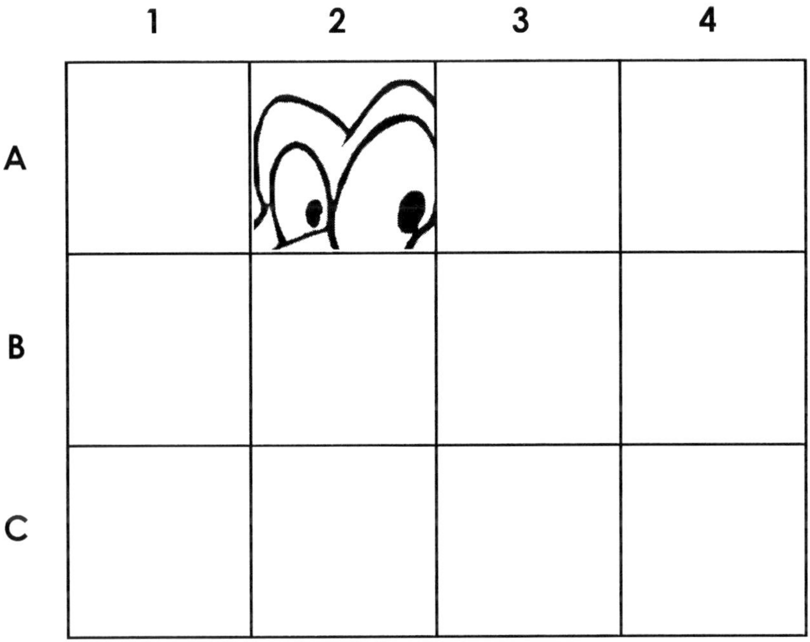
1
2
3
4
A
B
C

hangman

You'll need two or more players to play this game of hangman. Select one player to be the scribe, and the other player(s) will guess the phrase below. The scribe should look on page 82 to find the solution to the puzzle below.

LETTERS GUESSED

THE LORD COMMANDED THE ISRAELITES TO HAVE THIS TYPE OF DINNER EACH YEAR

___ ___ ___ ___ ___ ___ ___ ___

pick one

In each box, cross out all the letters that are repeated until only one remains. Place the remaining letter on the corresponding blank line at the bottom of the page. After you have done this for each box, you will find the answer to clue below. ***Solution on page 84.***

THE NUMBER OF YEARS THE CHILDREN OF ISRAEL SPENT IN THE WILDERNESS

4

F	L	H	B	I
I	S	K	S	L
H	B	F	K	T

2

G	E	B	J	C
X	O	U	X	E
C	U	J	B	G

5

E	T	W	C	P
A	Y	Z	A	Z
C	P	W	E	T

3

Z	V	K	I	L
F	O	R	F	O
I	L	Z	V	K

1

F	L	H	N	X
B	K	I	L	I
K	N	X	B	H

_____ _____ _____ _____ _____

1 2 3 4 5

word web

Follow the path below each letter until you reach the circle at the bottom of the page. Then write the letter in the circle. When you have done this for each letter, you will discover what Moses did for 40 days in order to grow closer to the Lord. ***Solution on page 85.***

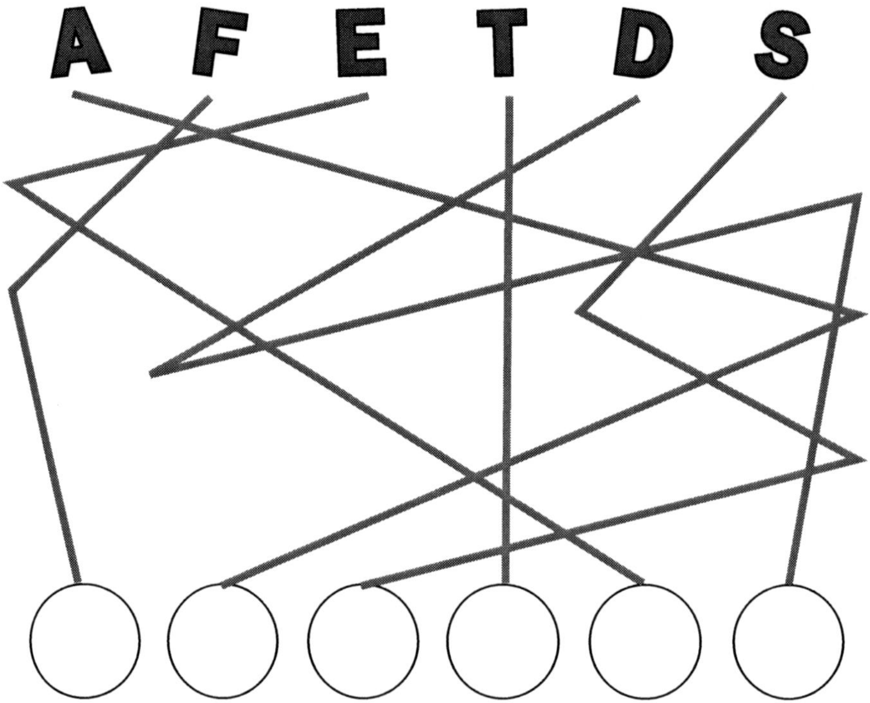

answer key

crossword puzzle

Genesis 11
ACROSS
3. EAST
5. CITY
6. BRICK
8. SLIME
10. RESTRAINED
11. HEAVEN

DOWN
1. LANGUAGE
2. SCATTERED
4. TOWER
5. CONFOUND
6. BABEL
7. CHILDREN
9. EARTH

Daniel 3
ACROSS
2. SHADRACH
6. BLESSED
7. FIRE
8. SERVE
11. FURNACE
12. GOD
14. POWER
15. NATION
16. MESHACH

DOWN
1. ABEDNEGO
2. SMELL
3. ANGEL
4. HIGH
5. WORSHIP
7. FOUR
9. HAIR
10. SERVANTS
13. DECREE

Exodus 20
ACROSS
2. SABBATH
5. DAUGHTER
7. HALLOWED
8. FATHER
10. GODS
13. GUILTLESS
14 LIKENESS

DOWN
1. COVET
2. SABBATH
3. ADULTERY
4. KILL
6. RESTED
9. WITNESS
11. STEAL
12. VAIN

Exodus 2
ACROSS
1. MOSES
4. NURSE
9. BULRUSHES
10. MOTHER
12. CHILD
14. THREE
15. DAUGHTER
16. HIDE

DOWN
2. SON
3. COMPASSION
5. RIVER
6. HEBREW
7. WATER
8. CHILD
11. SISTER
13. LEVI

Daniel 6
ACROSS
1. DELIVER
4. LIVE
6. WONDERS
9. COMMANDED
11. DEN
12. KING
13. POWER
16. LIVING
17. SERVANT
18. MORNING

DOWN
2. RESCUETH
3. TREMBLE
5. END
7. NATIONS
8. EARTH
10. DANIEL
12. KINGDOM
14. ANGEL
15. MOUTHS
16. LIONS

1 Kings 3
ACROSS
1. STRANGER
3. HALF
5. DIVIDE
7. DEAD
9. MORNING
11. GOD
12. SWORD
16. HOUSE
17. CHILD
18. ISRAEL
19. WOMEN
20. DIVIDE

DOWN
2. THIRD
4. LIVING
6. SON
8. DEAD
9. MIDNIGHT
10. MOTHER
11. GIVE
13. WISDOM
14. LIVING
15. CHILD

Malachi 4
ACROSS
2. RIGHTEOUSNESS
5. FATHERS
6. ROOT
9. SMITE
12. OVEN
13. HEALING
15. DAY
16. HEART
17. STUBBLE

DOWN
1. DREADFUL
3. CURSE
4. CHILDREN
7. ELIJAH
8. WICKED
10. ISRAEL
11. MOSES
14. LORD

---

hangman

PAGE 20
MELCHIZEDEK

PAGE 22
HEAVEN

PAGE 27
UR; EGYPT; CANAAN

PAGE 35
JACOB AND ESAU

PAGE 43
GOLDEN CALF

PAGE 48
TABERNACLE

PAGE 52
JOSHUA

PAGE 78
PASSOVER

dot-to-dot

PAGE 53

drawing from the scriptures

PAGE 69

PAGE 76

hidden message

PAGE 13

1. NEVER
2. FLOOD
3. THE
4. EARTH
5. AGAIN

missing letters

PAGE 8

1. GENESIS
2. EXODUS
3. LEVITICUS
4. NUMBERS
5. DEUTERONOMY

MOSES

PAGE 8

1. ASHER
2. BENJAMIN
3. DAN
4. GAD
5. ISSACHAR
6. JOSEPH
7. JUDAH
8. LEVI
9. NEPHTALI
10. REUBEN
11. SIMEON
12. ZEBULUN

mix n match

PAGE 24

Numbers 2 and 6 are the same.

PAGE 54

Numbers 3 and 10 are the same.

pick one

PAGE 12
KNOWLEDGE OF GOOD AND EVIL

PAGE 21
BRING ALL THE BROTHERS TO EGYPT

PAGE 38
ESTHER

PAGE 42
PUT LAMBS' BLOOD ON THEIR DOORS

PAGE 64
ALL THE DAYS OF HIS LIFE

PAGE 79
FORTY

secret code

1. BLESSINGS
2. COVENANTS
3. FAITH
4. FALL
5. IDOLATRY
6. LOYALTY
7. MARRIAGE
8. OBEDIENCE
9. PROPHECY
10. SACRIFICE

scripture chase

JEREMIAH

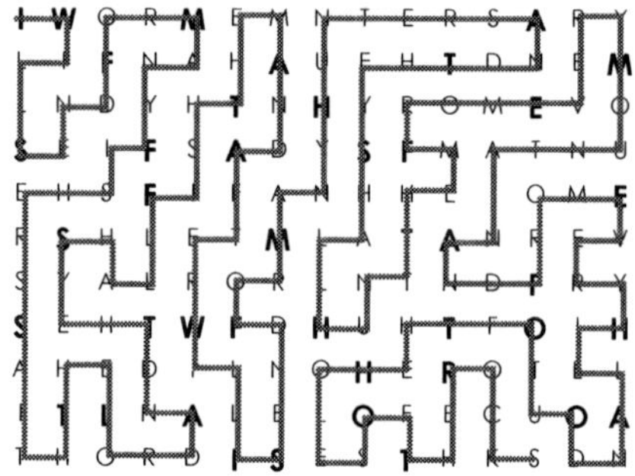

PSALM

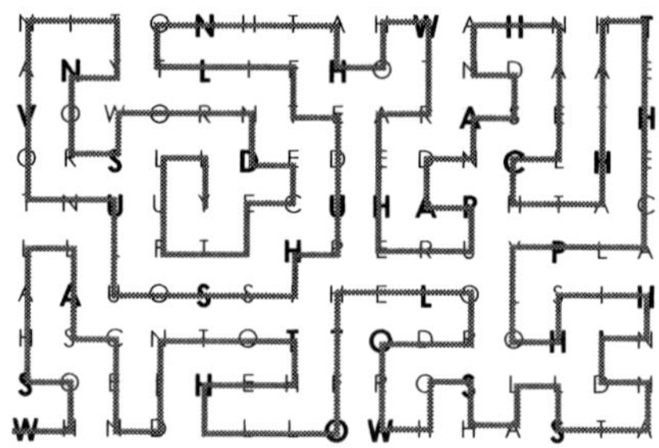

scripture puzzle

PAGE 10

Genesis 1:27

1. SO GOD
2. CREATED
3. MAN IN
4. HIS OWN
5. IMAGE
6. IN THE
7. IMAGE
8. OF GOD
9. CREATED
10. HE
11. HIM
12. MALE
13. AND
14. FEMALE
15. CREATED
16. HE
17. THEM

PAGE 32

Isaiah 53:3

1. HE IS
2. DESPISED
3. AND REJECTED
4. OF MEN
5. A MAN
6. OF SORROWS
7. AND ACQUAINTED
8. WITH GRIEF
9. AND WE HID
10. AS IT WERE
11. OUR FACES FROM HIM
12. HE WAS
13. DESPISED AND
14. WE ESTEEMED
15. HIM NOT

PAGE 46

Leviticus 19:18

1. THOU
2. SHALT NOT
3. AVENGE
4. NOR BEAR
5. ANY
6. GRUDGE
7. AGAINST
8. THE
9. CHILDREN
10. OF THY
11. PEOPLE BUT
12. THOU
13. SHALT
14. LOVE THY
15. NEIGHBOUR
16. AS THYSELF
17. I AM
18. THE
19. LORD

PAGE 58

Amos 3:7

1. SURELY
2. THE
3. LORD
4. GOD
5. WILL
6. DO
7. NOTHING
8. BUT
9. HE
10. REVEALETH
11. HIS
12. SECRET
13. UNTO
14. HIS
15. SERVANTS
16. THE
17. PROPHETS

---

word web

PAGE 16

LIGHT

PAGE 23

NAOMI

PAGE 26

EGYPT

PAGE 34

JORDAN

PAGE 80

FASTED

word search

PAGE 5

K	I	N	G	S	H	P	G	O	S	H	G	J	U	F
P	S	S	R	J	I	C	X	Y	P	T	X	T	T	Y
S	B	R	E	O	F	S	S	T	C	U	J	X	J	M
L	R	E	A	L	O	T	E	Q	G	R	W	S	H	T
A	E	B	Y	S	C	W	E	N	X	N	L	U	A	O
M	V	M	Q	E	R	I	M	H	E	G	B	M	I	S
S	O	U	H	K	X	Z	N	G	C	G	Z	J	M	M
Z	R	N	W	Y	M	O	N	O	R	E	T	U	E	D
J	P	H	P	J	Y	L	D	R	R	H	H	D	H	E
B	A	B	Y	O	R	U	W	U	E	H	G	G	E	P
Q	L	E	O	B	K	S	U	P	S	H	C	E	N	M
B	U	S	U	C	I	T	I	V	E	L	T	S	S	M
L	E	U	M	A	S	W	V	N	Y	J	Z	S	R	V
H	X	G	E	C	C	L	E	S	I	A	S	T	E	S
G	A	R	Z	E	K	I	J	O	S	H	U	A	K	R

PAGE 7

E	J	Z	O	O	Q	T	G	D	H	S	G	J	D	J
Z	U	I	G	A	M	O	S	T	A	O	T	D	O	Q
N	V	J	C	D	H	O	S	E	A	N	I	E	X	M
A	W	J	I	S	A	I	A	H	D	G	I	G	G	A
H	Z	E	P	H	A	N	I	A	H	O	H	E	W	L
U	T	J	E	J	H	R	V	H	A	F	A	O	L	A
M	I	D	H	Z	B	D	C	O	F	S	B	B	N	C
R	F	J	E	R	E	M	I	A	H	O	A	A	L	H
U	O	V	J	C	W	K	F	G	J	L	K	D	K	I
M	I	C	A	H	L	E	I	Q	O	O	K	I	A	D
R	R	N	B	L	I	C	S	E	E	M	U	A	V	K
P	Z	V	J	O	N	A	H	A	L	O	K	H	M	D
M	Z	E	C	H	A	R	I	A	H	N	T	F	G	O
L	A	M	E	N	T	A	T	I	O	N	S	R	F	Q
R	C	C	N	V	J	M	I	H	A	G	G	A	I	P

PAGE 31

W	L	J	D	S	S	I	C	A	I	N	R	M	R	S
A	E	M	A	A	A	X	T	C	H	M	A	V	I	C
U	H	W	O	G	V	M	O	T	T	L	O	E	S	H
F	C	A	I	G	P	I	U	E	R	L	Y	S	A	M
H	A	N	N	A	H	R	D	E	X	E	Q	O	A	U
P	R	X	N	Q	L	A	M	W	L	B	N	W	C	G
W	G	M	Z	A	M	Z	I	N	S	A	O	D	N	M
I	J	V	D	X	S	N	E	A	W	K	E	O	O	I
E	C	L	E	N	Y	U	U	O	B	L	R	L	H	I
V	Z	P	L	A	N	L	V	L	I	A	A	V	T	G
E	X	K	U	O	O	W	T	L	A	S	I	Z	A	P
F	W	D	C	M	Q	W	A	D	B	P	D	U	I	E
Q	W	F	F	I	C	H	C	A	G	S	A	I	L	E
W	L	Z	H	A	E	L	O	L	Y	X	S	H	O	J
P	I	M	U	O	R	H	T	E	J	L	R	H	G	Q

PAGE 37

U	R	Y	W	T	I	B	H	B	B	S	O	Y	R	R
C	C	W	U	W	S	N	A	L	E	U	N	A	K	A
R	B	R	L	V	R	M	D	D	T	O	E	Z	X	I
D	E	B	U	R	A	Y	U	Q	H	Y	D	G	M	O
N	W	V	A	O	E	T	J	S	L	E	E	N	O	Z
A	D	O	I	B	L	B	F	S	E	A	F	I	A	N
L	G	O	A	R	Y	Z	O	O	H	R	O	N	B	Z
D	A	L	N	Y	N	L	M	N	E	T	N	E	B	V
E	C	J	I	O	G	A	O	H	M	H	E	V	I	V
S	N	E	S	X	C	R	D	N	Q	S	D	E	N	E
I	A	R	T	H	C	E	G	R	T	K	R	H	E	Z
M	A	I	N	S	W	D	N	G	O	Z	A	D	V	D
O	N	C	U	E	Y	S	I	U	Q	J	G	M	A	J
R	A	H	O	V	W	E	K	Z	T	P	Y	G	E	N
P	C	O	M	E	L	A	S	U	R	E	J	C	H	G

PAGE 45

Z	B	H	K	T	I	T	H	E	S	Z	V	O	W	K
D	L	T	X	T	Z	D	D	N	A	T	I	O	N	J
E	E	C	G	Z	M	H	O	U	S	E	X	F	Y	X
F	S	T	O	R	E	H	O	U	S	E	X	C	Y	W
H	S	X	H	T	E	H	F	T	T	S	U	B	O	I
K	I	Q	Z	Z	Z	R	Y	L	W	F	W	A	F	L
U	N	U	V	I	U	R	O	O	M	C	X	H	F	F
X	G	B	R	O	H	H	D	T	W	P	V	D	E	Y
U	O	A	P	O	S	N	C	A	M	R	R	O	R	Y
R	K	J	F	U	I	E	C	O	E	O	Z	M	I	B
P	L	F	W	W	T	Y	F	N	W	V	V	H	N	E
C	F	O	J	C	U	R	S	E	S	E	K	P	G	V
V	Y	H	I	B	Z	Z	P	L	O	R	D	C	S	O
E	I	X	H	Q	Q	W	M	E	A	T	W	K	C	S
S	A	X	A	G	A	B	A	S	Q	A	I	P	U	F

1. ROB
2. TITHES
3. OFFERINGS
4. CURSE
5. NATION
6. STOREHOUSE
7. MEAT
8. HOUSE
9. PROVE
10. LORD
11. WINDOWS
12. POUR
13. BLESSINGS
14. ROOM

PAGE 57

U	G	H	T	L	T	M	R	H	C	Y	Q	R	D	X
C	M	O	U	G	K	T	P	H	I	L	L	D	G	A
C	X	T	N	I	O	Z	Y	S	Y	W	A	C	Q	D
W	P	B	E	E	D	S	Y	O	P	M	E	Y	R	K
B	C	Z	L	X	V	R	G	O	L	D	O	N	A	U
Y	G	B	H	W	C	A	E	Z	S	C	W	N	R	B
U	S	S	U	R	E	P	E	A	W	C	Y	Q	A	V
T	Y	G	R	C	G	C	I	H	M	N	D	F	D	X
T	F	N	S	N	K	R	Y	B	V	L	J	N	V	G
S	U	I	I	P	O	Z	Y	M	Z	Q	A	V	S	G
D	W	K	Q	F	I	Y	Q	R	M	T	C	R	X	J
N	P	E	O	P	L	E	D	U	S	H	T	E	N	S
A	O	V	W	M	I	E	N	O	T	S	T	V	E	W
H	F	Y	L	Z	T	G	T	S	P	J	Y	E	U	M
C	N	N	L	N	L	S	I	X	S	T	K	N	Y	S

1. KINGS
2. HEAVEN
3. NEVER
4. PEOPLE
5. STAND
6. STONE
7. HANDS
8. CLAY
9. GOLD
10. DREAM
11. SURE

0 26575 53689 8